Grid

Brenda Schmidt

HAGIOS PRESS

Library and Archives Canada Cataloguing in Publication

Schmidt, Brenda, 1965–
    Grid / Brenda Schmidt.

Poems.
ISBN 978-1-926710-13-6

    I. Title.

PS8587.C45588G75 2012   C811'.6   C2012-901523-7

Edited by Paul Wilson.
Designed and typeset by Donald Ward.
Cover art: "Drive-1," reduction woodcut print by Lee A
    McKay.
Cover design by Tania Wolk, Go Giraffe Go Inc.
Set in Minion Pro.
Printed and Bound in Canada.

The publishers gratefully acknowledge the assistance of the Saskatchewan Arts Board and The Canada Council for the Arts in the production of this book.

HAGIOS PRESS
Box 33024 Cathedral PO
Regina SK   S4T 7X2
www.hagiospress.com

for Harvey

Contents

MIDWAY

The Photo Lab 8
An Exercise in Perspective 9
Riverbank Lines 10
Morning in the Park, Reading *Scientific American
  Mind* 12
A Note to Joy 13
What We Wish For 14
What Next 15
Midway 16
All Hail the Disenchantment Thesis 17
Horsing Around 8
This is My Brain on Birds 19
Express Lane, *American Scientist* in Hand 21
Overflowing 22
Wren 23
Dear Li Po 24
Nine Ways to Woo a Bug Photographer 25
Warts and All 28
Some Progress 29

CORRIDOR

Mystic Lake Road Corridor 32

ROAD CONDITIONS

Leaves 42
Whiteout 43
Suet 45
Course of Treatment 46
Fort 48
After the Storm 49

O Whirlybird   50
Barometric   51
Small Song for a Slippery Road   52
Funeral Plans   53
As We Hold Each Other   54
Too Far   55

GRID

Great Blue Heron   58
A Field of Round Bales   59
Yes Bobolinks   60
Grid   62
Tripod   63
Standing in Canola   64
To Those Considering a Return to the Land   65
Constellation   66
Black Terns   67
Endangered   68
Bone Coulee   69
Fledgling   70
Jones' Peak   71
Who Gets What   72
Local Anesthetic   73
Visiting Hours   74
Stroke   75
Webs in the Graveyard   76
Love, the Dance   77

Acknowledgements   79

Midway

THE PHOTO LAB

The line-up is long. Just one checkout open.
Ahead, a woman goes through shot after shot:

grandchildren, their children; a little girl hugging
a dog, tractor in the background, steel bin, blue sky,

the photographer's long shadow. Were Darwin
alive and in line he'd nod at the investment,

at the typical machine, the long line of genes.
I read that the brain processes faces more easily

when they're right-side up. Orientation is everything.
So much for alternate positions. People come and go

through automatic doors. We become our inventions.
The line-up remains. Faces change. The guy behind

digs into the Rip-L chips as we shuffle ahead
with our appetites. Greasy fingers. Snaps

slip into an envelope, the origin glossy side up
like it matters. It might. I can almost taste the salt.

AN EXERCISE IN PERSPECTIVE

Wired to eat the web spun
over time, spin another
just the same. Wait for vibration.
Under the porch light a spider
darts on the edge of darkness
feet from our heads, her silver
path scarce visible, quivering
like a lip. I hate you.
Hate just slipped. Its silk
stuck to a wall. Sticks
to everything. Later it will stick
to the sheets. Under the stars
we grow old before our time
in our stable orbits, cores dense,
glaring, gravitationally bound
by a mass of past arguments,
neither noiseless or patient.
Whitman knew better the lengths
to which one goes to connect.
To stand isolated. Further east
researchers measure
the output of a spider's heart
in a lab, observe the contractions,
while mine beats into the night
unnoticed and untouched.
I ought to be grateful. Here
the orb weaver gives us
her daily web, forgives us
our stare.

RIVERBANK LINES

Riverbank Lines, Dorothy Knowles, 2006. Charcoal
drawing on paper.

Where the waves meet the bank it's light
as the scar on my bikini line.
A few quick strokes
wet the sand.

§

This is where I'll spread
the blanket, anchor
the corners with rocks.
The wind today is a friend
who wants to sleep
with my enemy. Forget
the umbrella.

§

The river delivers,
gust after gust. It's a wonder
anything stays rooted.
Just beyond a nodding-thistle
once stood, me beside,
Wildflowers Across the Prairies
in hand, its pages white flags flapping,
the plant, tall as me, bending
like me, agreeing with everything,
stems spineless, going by the book.

§

Gulls bob on the waves
before me, moments
of confidence all facing
the same direction, never
drawing close to shore.

§

Shear stress on the bank
will be greater after days of rain.
The river has never been higher.
The bank, as I see it, is a short course
on erosion, what it means to let go,
to look outward. It's a blackboard,
an ecologist's equation
where 2s become 7s
when tramped with flip-flops.

§

The riverbank is a memory bank. Here
a flock of Black-bellied Plovers rested,
one Ruddy Turnstone among them.
The next day they were gone
so I stored the empty shore
and looked elsewhere.

MORNING IN THE PARK,
READING *SCIENTIFIC AMERICAN MIND*

Place-tracking neurons and multiple grids
all operate in my head somewhere
near the hippocampus. While I sit. Kids
run by. The rats studied likely didn't care
to run like that in their cages, all wired
with electrodes, not on sugar or caffeine.
I'm up to here with spatial data, tired
of the racket. Brats. The older ones lean
bikes against the monkey bars, climb, then swing,
screaming, from rung to rung, untied laces
dangling. A girl runs from her mom, clutching
a half-clothed doll, squealing, making faces
on my behalf. Dear GPS in my head:
show me the quickest path back to bed.

A NOTE TO JOY

Stop by. I'll be around.
Today you'd find me reeking

of DEET in a plastic Adirondack,
nearing the end of *Human Wishes*,

waving now and then at mosquitoes,
naming the ones that land after

diseases they inject then . . . Splat!
Life sticks to my hand. Imagine,

as a child I'd watch the mosquito
fill with my blood. I felt needed.

Joy, I always felt your touch whenever
a mosquito withdrew and flew off.

I'd spend hours wondering where
I'd end up. Now dragonflies

catch their wings on the rosebush
behind me. Swallows rip into fullness

further up, change direction in a hurry,
wings pointed as the results of a government

funded study. I'll swat another, think again
about heading in. I want to believe

scientists are this close to pinpointing
the gene that carried you away.

WHAT WE WISH FOR

A Girl, Ron Mueck, 2006.

So there it is, naked as can be,
great compliment to the pain
stored in the mind's nursery and the pain
is nothing compared to the fear.
This newborn is a warning of the size,
the enormity, of what lies
ahead. Her 14-odd feet multiplied
by fear equals the rest of one's life, highs
and lows, all glossed, taken into account.
The folds of her eyelids and labia seem
evil. Mean. Impossibly clean.
Is this what we wish for? Tantamount
to faith, that oversized mould we pour ourselves
into. Mine is cracked, the clay maquette shelved.

WHAT NEXT

On and on he goes. Something about
chipper-shredders. Gas or electric.
Coffee's going down. Sheets
a mess. Too early to make
heavy-duty decisions.
He puts the blind up, goes on,
the sun a day-old chick
through the foggy condensation.
Triple pane's a pain
when the seal lets go. Clarity
depends on a gas-filled space.
Insulated glazing. We're at the point
where everything is just past warranty.
Now we barely make out
the shapes of oncoming robins.
And sparrows? Forget it. He goes on,
something about sticks and what
rocks do to tungsten blades,
as I point out what might be
a flock of waxwings. Over they go,
unheard.

MIDWAY

Not a small town ride
I'd ever pay to be on, yet
I watched it come round with all

its dents, in want of paint,
alive to that one click of metal.
It came after the cotton candy;

the matter of starting
a family. I think pink yet
see only vague charcoal smudges

moving to the right, charcoal
clowns, a charcoal Ferris wheel
turning, empty charcoal seats.

It didn't come while we stood
on the sidewalk, the oncoming
question riding with toddlers

on the backs of cream Shetlands.
It came after dark. After
the rain began, after the head-down

scramble to the car,
slamming of doors,
slap of the wipers.

I buckled up
knowing the question
had been left behind.

ALL HAIL THE DISENCHANTMENT THESIS

The thunder was the ghost of a golfer shouting *Fore!*
as someone will later say, from the rough of the eternal
PGA tournament, for everyone in the parking lot,
the girl in the pink dress with the grape popsicle,
the girl in white, without, watching her lick,
the pony-tailed mom with baby harnessed to her chest,
the old man rattling the coin slot on the shopping cart,
two pre-teens, hands squared with silvery devices,
the baying beagle in the minivan, the greasy-eyed poodle
eying the Ring-billed Gull, legs the colour of speed bumps,
then the boy with baggy shorts on the too-small bike,
stopped and looked up into the fall line,
the cold pause, the continuous present, until hail
the size of earbuds smacked flesh, if not souls,
pelted the pavement, the cars, bouncing like pop culture
references must in a plastic mind, through time, bouncing
off windshields, rear-view mirrors, at unpredictable angles,
dinging doors, spokes, the roofs of stores, and now
golf ball-sized, as they'll say on the news, potentially
lethal, and everyone is spectator and spectacle,
terminal velocity explained, history down cold,
down to a science, the evolution of running, screaming,
the physics of slamming doors, the metaphysical shielding
with upturned hands, a *good God, sweet Jesus,* the scene
deranged, a driving range, a missile range, inevitable
war, a brief engagement of white with a little purple.

HORSING AROUND

Somehow during our walk horses came up,
the kind we rode through childhood.
H drew a line in the dirt, shook the invisible
reins and galloped off down the road,
tall as Hoss Cartwright, my *Bonanza*,
feet cum hooves, riding flat-out,
slapping to make his horse gallop faster.
Gallop it did. O, those hindquarters!
I nudged my nag a few times before it budged.
It bucked a bit, reared up, then took off.
I galloped down the homestretch, slapping my ass.
What are the odds? But there we were,
after all these years of fighting
for position, a long shot hugging the rail,
H ahead by several lengths and pulling away.

THIS IS MY BRAIN ON BIRDS

A family of chickadees murmurs in the willow
by the window and I think the lobes of my brain
must be black-capped, white-cheeked, dark-
legged with claws that cling to the centre
of a nervous system, lobes too limited
in my cranium, so they flew off with faith
in the sky, a skull that will remain intact,
no matter how hard the fall, pressure aside,
in spite of the atmosphere. What nonsense
a lonely soul finds when looking. It's dangerous
to think the surface gravity of a relationship
means it's grounded, but for a time a force
held us together and we sat on the iron bench
beneath the trees while the wings of unseen
birds brushed the leaves and we identified each
by its song. You had the better ear, knew all
the calls. I listened for years to finally hear
what you did, learned the notes only make sense
once you attend to them, like when the chickadee
I'll call the frontal lobe repeats *cheeseburger
cheeseburger*, the way I would *love* if convinced
it's more than mnemonic, not just some word
picked at random in a language I'll never understand.
The parietal lobe hangs upside down like my life
will once you're gone, my fears realized.
It picks at a bug or seed I cannot see, then
looks at me as if it's my job to hold out
a handful of peanuts and focus on the grip
I lack in comparison, the lack of vision,
what happens when a nut isn't shelled.
The occipital lobe lags behind, slow to get
moving, as if freshly emerged from the dream
that has been bothering me all morning,

now and then stretching its wings, extending
one leg backward, *free me* escaping a bill
straight and sharp as the point you made
about commitment and what it might mean
to come home. What home means. *Free me.*
The temporal lobe, meanwhile, hops madly
from branch to branch, peering in the fissures
I hadn't noticed. Some shallow, some not. Given
the chance I'd show you those gaps edged with bark.

EXPRESS LANE, *AMERICAN SCIENTIST* IN HAND

Yes, I'm trying too hard to impress you,
I nearly say to the man in front who's looking
down at me and the cover, and yes, I'll read
about the genetic tug-of war, plug-in
hybrids and prehistoric hurricanes, then go
put on something pretty. Yes, a one-track mind
takes up part of this issue. Wait, I bet you think
I'm buying this mag for my husband
like some well-trained, perfect-plain domestic
dream who buys romaine and makes her own croutons.
Note the bag of nuts among my less-than-10 items.
They're for me. I've been known to crunch them.

OVERFLOWING

Downpours seldom get to me,
but after I hung up, rain
filled the troughs and a little tree
washed over. Likely a maple.
Next time you call I'll tell you
the seedling had arms, I swear,
that flapped madly as it fell,
its brief scream ending
somewhere between
the daylily and the bleeding
heart and man it's so
good to hear your voice.

WREN

The nest under the eave is unfinished,
the pile of twigs a messy affair.
You pointed it out and later I came back,
looked up at it, at the sun on the sticks,
wondering if a cup nest in that mess could
hold the future. A spider sac was all I saw.
Nothing built at that angle could survive
a storm and sure enough one came.
The wren must have felt the coming
thunder in the quills of its feathers
for it perched on the fence this morning
and pitched its song in that direction,
the initial notes a clear, almost faithful
translation of "Visit" in *Birthday Letters,*
though perhaps too compressed, the rest
a volley of rocks against the window
my heart keeps closed. The glass broke
of course, shattered inward, and strong gusts
filled the room the way gods fill books, the wind pushed
the bedroom door open, the shadows of clouds
travelling across the duvet as if it were the world
and time a high thread count, the cotton smooth
as your lips in the light of the vineyard
in Cypress Hills the other day. They met
the glass like friends as you tasted each wine,
going from dry to sweetest, cleansing your palate
in-between, while I, attuned to the singing of the glass,
went from sober to forever thirsty and there, too,
in the landscape altered beyond belief, was singing.

DEAR LI PO,

The birch in the backyard
snapped last night in the storm,
the top ten feet now borne
by the willow like a coffin.
Yesterday a Dark-eyed Junco
pursued another beneath it,
tail spread wide, the outer
feathers on each side forming
elongated hearts
that touched the branches.

NINE WAYS TO WOO A BUG PHOTOGRAPHER

1.

Leave no upside-down beetle unturned.
Perfect the art of capture. All it takes
is a jar and a piece of paper. Remember
the legs are vulnerable when pedaling
the air like that. There's a reason it's lying
on its back, so be gentle. Mind the antennae
while it feels things out. Not all beetles
feel the same. It's not as hard as it looks.

2.

Keep the broom away from the web
in the hallway. Sweep around it.
Let the dust settle on the silk.
Say it's in memory of Charlotte.

3.

Look into the eye of the satin moth.
Perfectly lit. A flash diffuser prevents
unwanted reflections. A clear image
requires even light. Understand
it could never be more even than this.
The depth of field is dependant
on focal length and tends to be
shallow so don't be surprised
when you see the screen.
The background will be blurry.

4.

Follow a mayfly at the low level crossing.
Ask which of the 611 known species
of the US and Canada it could be.
Wonder aloud how much of its day remains.

5.

Spot a golden crab spider on a wild rose,
its legs like wide-held arms
waiting for a grandchild's hug.
It will hold that pose until prey comes along.

6.

Hand over the limp toadflax
you pulled from the garden.
Point to the tiny spotted beetle
nose down between the bloom's lips.

7.

Gesture wordlessly
at the moult of a dragonfly
clutching a reed at Table Creek.
Nod when you're later told
it's from an American
Emerald. Remain wordless
when you find that cast
skin of emptiness splitting
next to the thyme in the sun room.

8.

When all else fails, wear white
so you resemble the sunny side
of a house. Sometimes being
mistaken for a wall is what it takes
to entice the hairy flower beetle to land.

9.

Spend the evening hunting for a tree cricket
in the trees along the road, the continuous trill
a rubbing of wings. As a rule, the hotter it is
the faster the chirp. Follow your ear
carefully to the alder or to some plant
you cannot name and when the song stops
lift the holey leaf it uses as a megaphone.
Underneath you'll find the one rubbing.

WARTS AND ALL

The rainbow toad, believed to be extinct,
made headlines in the BBC Nature News
this morning, *beautiful* the word used
in the story, an image of a living
specimen backing up the claim, and who,
after rediscovering a passion deep in the night,
one thought lost, could view that rough body
and not recognize the colours, not wonder
if a team of prior selves, a multitude as Pessoa
would have it, had mounted an expedition
through the mountain forest of the past,
shining lights on the highest branches until
a beam caught an eye, the skin, found the warts
merely wart-like, the precise spectrum
seen when the head tilts back with a moan.

SOME PROGRESS

It's all gone: the overturned
pickup, cab crushed, wheels missing,
undercarriage rusted and dusty.
Crouching beside it was the panel van
with missing front end, there
for a good year or more. On the west side
a Volvo BM loader sat idle,
one rear tire flat. It leaned in,
snuggled up to a Case track hoe.

We focus on the foxtail, the clover, plan holidays,
until we reach the highway, where we turn
around and head back home, half-way
through our recommended daily weight-bearing
activity. Blood pressure's down. Pictures of health.
This is where we pause for a moment.
Who wouldn't. Directly across the blacktop

the great wall of the tailings pond grows
ever higher. On it track hoes and trucks
look like toys. Warning signs
tell us to do the obvious.
On the south-facing slope
the test patch of grass is greener
than the average lawn.
Part of the enhancement phase.
It keeps the dust down.

Corridor

MYSTIC LAKE ROAD CORRIDOR

1.

We find the waypoint
where the Black-throated

Green Warbler sang
three years ago.

That point in time
a point in space

we keep seeking,
a black dot

on a grey screen.
We watch

ourselves approaching
the spot: aerial view

in real time,
a slow-moving star

on a long curve,
small,

midway,
closing in.

2.

Bread, brie. Overhead a Ruby-
Crowned Kinglet. Listen. Let it say,

I've been where you've been. Let it say,
I know where you grew up. That it's possible

it bears an atom of you. Or will. Or not.
Listen. It repeats. It sings the rock,

sings bog. Sings the bread
down your throat.

3.

Crouching just off the road. Bog
rosemary in bud. Some already open.

A truck slows. I wave,
hold my breath. It keeps going

and I am enveloped, filmed,
a whim, all eyes,

quick glances, bits of pink,
drooping blooms

the faces of tiny dolls
weeping.

4.

Hermit Thrush. Tail bobbing
in the clearing. Reddish

lifts of light. In the sights:
eye ring, head tilted. Hunting—

all this hunting, searching,
for something, for nothing,

for distance, for some place
on Darwin's tree—a perch, a dead

branch, a vantage. High interest. Ahead
some coherence. Decisions, decisions.

Looking through a forest, a paradox,
through binoculars, high-end optics

through language, DNA, with senses,
with pretense,

with each other. Yes,
it depends.

It will depend.

5.

All this singing. O, the ambience.
Ovenbird. Myrtle just ahead.

A waterthrush over yonder.
Look. Over yonder,

Mystic. Woodsworth Bay.
Almost Romantic.

To think *An Evening Walk*
would somehow lead

to a *Carbon Shift*. *Sea Sick*. But here
we are. The books

whip back like branches. Smack.
It's stinging. The switch,

has it happened? Maybe.
It's June and May is still here.

On the same trail, beaten,
Woodsworth still a ways away,

bits of blue through leaves.
Woods, not words. Wait,

this cannot be the present tense.
The Ovenbird has stopped singing.

When did the Ovenbird stop singing?

6.

Tundra Swans on Mystic Creek. So white
dabbling in their calm

reflections, dabbling in the inverted trees.
We keep our distance.

Through binoculars it shrinks.
And the whiteness lessens.

I focus on their curves. All
five necks slide in and out of Mystic, in

and out of view. All five necks
look dirty. Impure.

They're immature, you say. Sure.
I flip through Sibley, find the words:

first summer
and one calls out

while I'm reading, as if
my eyes are playing

the words in the guide.
The music is wheezy, melancholy, clear,

and I
identify.

7.

Bear tracks in the mud at the curve
past McLeans. An inside toe missing.

Yet squint just right and the impression
might be there. The road, after all, is drying.

It was heading the way I came. It's heavy and I
won't follow. I stand downwind on the sun

side, let my shadow fall beside the tracks.
Raise a hand. Raise the camera. Click.

Self-portrait: *Bear with Me,*
a picture anyone can see, if anyone bothers

looking for a track among tracks,
a shadow among so many shadows.

8.

The bear tracks mud from the curve
through the corridor in mind. It leads to a girl.

She can't imagine looking through the stink of bear
for bears. For the mortal soul. The moat

the girl wishes for as she walks along
has no stomach, smells of nothing,

its stone bridge doesn't support a wall
of tourists, their eyes behind

viewfinders, looking down
on what is forced to pace a space

so narrow and sunless. The girl
kicks ridges in a summerfallow field.

Looks ahead. Smells the dust the wind
swipes westward towards a shack of dreams

to come, a shack in a hollow, a bedroom, a mess.
There. A whiff of tansy. Forgive her.

In the field she's alone, collecting
little rocks unearthed by her feet.

Limestone, she loves limestone, rocks
she wets with spit to better see

fossils. Colours. Mineral sparkle.
In this way she resembles

the woman on a castle bridge
across the ocean, bears below, the woman

who licks a finger and runs it over
the wall's stone.

9.

Near the curve, bending down, stroking
the moss on the limestone, getting between it

and the quiet sun. I know it's quiet now.
Know scientists plot sunspots, deep calm.

Solar minimum in the news
again. And again I bend, killing

batteries, trying to capture all this
life, whatever's emerging, dying, lost,

suspecting all the while the lens
is smeared, shutter slow, pictures

blurry. Still I stumble among fallen
beauty. Falling all the time. Mindful

of crevices, tricks of light, Sontag, potential
fractures, image stabilization, whatever's

framed and literal. Quiet now.
Hold steady. The camera has its limits.

Road Conditions

LEAVES

Storm stayed. Days away
from saying our goodbyes.

Cheek against the window,
purposely looking east

as if focusing
on this cardinal point

will keep him alive
long enough for us to get there.

For hours I focus on the leaves.
January and so many leaves

still clinging to the trees—
mountain ash, willow, alder,

maple, poplar, birch—
twisted, shriveled, shivering,

as if they didn't quite know
how to go about falling.

WHITEOUT

Dying for an end to this
howling wind, zero visibility.

Where the earth and sky might meet
it's white as toilet paper,

the horizon wiped out.
We're not going anywhere.

Check road conditions, road
closures, listen to the news.

Coronach, Rockglen, and Kincaid
still without power. Lines down,

poles snapped, crews hampered
by blizzard conditions. Stranded

motorists. Another lost soul
who headed out on foot

didn't make it. When you're cold
to the bone, the farmhouse is further

away than it appears. Inside strangers
wrapped in printed blankets

tune in to CBC, the static,
sit near candles, flickering

illusions of smiles
on expressionless faces,

premium polar fleece
wolves at their throats,

eyes fuzzy and fixed on
the design of the weather.

SUET

The mountain ash outside
looks exactly like the tree
behind Brother Leo in the black-
and-white illustration opening
the chapter "Of Perfect Joy"
in *The Little Flowers
of St. Francis of Assisi*, the Book-
of-the-Month Club edition.
Minus the leaves. I find snow
among the words in the cold
passage that follows, feel stuck
as ever. The day drags
a knotted branch around.
Magpies come and go, ripping
the suet I leave hanging
near the trunk. Beef fat
from the Co-op, no charge,
stuffed in a green wire cage.
I'm an animal. Waiting
is a bill that picks
through frozen ribs.

COURSE OF TREATMENT

When the thyroid goes to hell
it takes everything with it,

even half of each eyebrow. It's possible
two of every 100 people pencil them in

each morning before heading to work,
energy permitting. The gland sits in the neck

like a White Admiral, wings spread
in the sun, until a bird picks it off,

feeds it to the brood. When winter comes,
bloodwork. Didn't even notice when

the needle slipped in, the results barely
registered. It's been 40 below forever. So

begins a daily dose of thyroxine
and each day snow

becomes deeper, the drifts harder,
the trees more stark. Today

as the male Pine Grosbeak peeks in,
crushing one sunflower seed

after another, its feathers
begin to separate.

Now its breast
puffs out, red-faced,

a little girl bawling
in a toy isle

before a breath
holding episode.

FORT

In time the girl will learn a blizzard
has to meet certain conditions

before it can own its name.
In time she'll call it as she does her dog

when it disappears on the other
side of the bale stack. She knows

dogs will dig for mice forever
and it's time to go in, dry her mitts,

sit on the register. She knows
the bus won't come tomorrow,

the roads blocked, that homework
will eventually arrive by skidoo

along with enough groceries to see them
through. She knows tomorrow

she'll dig a snow fort, hollow it out,
admire the thin blue roof, the shovel

standing guard at the entrance, the dog
christening the only way out.

AFTER THE STORM

A few redpolls chase
birch seed over the drifts,
while the majority hunker
down in the feeders. I am
your basic fast food fly thru.
Bought two bags of black oil
sunflower seed so far, 20 kg
each. Their appetites show
no signs of slowing. Before
sunrise I bundled up, shoveled
a path, filled everything.
The beauty routine
temporarily diminishing the wrinkles
in my plans. Inside I look hard
through binoculars
at the undertail coverts to tell
the Common from the Hoary.
Sometimes there's no telling
this close to spring. Who knew
the shit of such tiny birds
could throw up so much steam?

O WHIRLYBIRD

You groan through the night
as if riveted

to the rust-free metal
of intractable pain,

the dull aluminum
flashing.

Curved vanes
deflect everything,

remove excess
moisture from our attic.

The constant spin
improves efficiency,

prevents the build-up
of ice.

With ball bearings
lubricated,

guaranteed for life,
you vent.

BAROMETRIC

At the weather office, checking
the current conditions. A headache.

Can't think straight. Can't get
Gordon Lightfoot out of my head.

If You Could Read My Mind.
There he is sucking strawberry

Boost through a white straw
like he did last night in my dreams,

coughing and blowing bubbles
while reading erroneous reports

of his death. I rushed to his side,
worried he might choke,

saw roads through the stubble,
ruts in his lips then

recognized the greyness, the storm
I can't wait out.

SMALL SONG FOR A SLIPPERY ROAD

The highway is a crack
in that cold white wall,

red flags at the curve
where it heaves

heedless drivers into space
less traveled.

There's one set of tracks
before me, one lane

cleared. My traction depends
on the salt and sand

spread by the driver
of that big yellow truck.

Its red lights flash high
above the swirl ahead.

I slow and follow. Thank God
for the Department of Highways.

FUNERAL PLANS

Plan ahead. That's key,
we agree as we watch

the just-shoveled driveway
fill like a grave. Funerals are big

business, you say as the plough
heads up the street,

leaving a ridge that will take
forever to clear away.

Like ploughs, we go on even though
we've had this conversation before,

long ago pushing away the ritual.
Coffins are traps. Don't let the wolves

profit on your grief. Keep it simple:
cremate, spread the ashes

as you would a shovelful of snow.

AS WE HOLD EACH OTHER

The shadow of the maple
spiders past

the house, ends
in the driveway.

It makes no sense,
but we hold the length of it

in our gaze anyway, as if
depth could be gained

from a shadow punctured
at some point by a fox, a girl,

snow slipping from lines,
winter tires.

TOO FAR

The one road out is longer after a cold stretch.
Iced-over hydro lines hang
like skipping ropes
from a childhood that never goes away.
Cinderella dressed in white
went downstairs to say goodnight.
Made a blunder.
Too far under.
How many shovels make it right?
None. The going is slow, conditions poor, traffic
steady. There's a shovel in every trunk.

§

Lots of tracks in the ditch.
This is where we saw the caribou
but that was back in the summer
before the roads got slippery, before
the ditches filled. The two ran along
the tree line, heading toward us, as if
they'd just heard they were endangered,
their habitat in decline, as if
they felt they still had a chance
and made a run for it.

§

A coyote stares as we pass. I don't blame it.
71000 lost their paws in Saskatchewan
last season, last I read. *Promise me:*
if my luck runs out on this stretch

do not erect a cross. No coyote
needs to lift its leg in memory.
Shake on it.
Snow starts to fall.

§

Can barely see the ditch for the ice
on the window. *Where in hell*
is the scraper? I use my nails.
Through the scratch marks
the forest resembles a bit of parsley
left on the cutting board.
Two hours in, we veer south,
the silence between us thick as soup.

§

Outside The Pas we spot a Great Grey Owl
in the spruce. As we slow it looks up
like a doctor might from a chart with bad news.
You have to wonder. Down the road
another in hunting position, eyes locked
on four feet of snow, where a vole must be,
the furry matter of survival. *Too far under.*

Grid

GREAT BLUE HERON

(after viewing the murals by Count Berthold Von Imhoff in St. Peter's Cathedral)

In a creek,
hunting in the evening light.

I stare at the ditch for miles,
imagining Imhoff

applying coat after coat of paint
to each feather, gold leaf to its bill

leaving it poised in the creek
for eternity,

a saint who lifts
every time a car slows.

We kept going.
We're on our way home,

wasting no time.
Not a word.

The heron never moves.

A FIELD OF ROUND BALES

A field of minds
entwined.

The field of shrinking
shrinks.

A wanderer's
possessions

lost.

A field of beads
on a sod slipper.

A field of toes
poking out.

YES BOBOLINKS

Memories flutter like Bobolinks in a hayfield
along the access road to a semi-ghost town.
I noticed them on the way into Robsart yesterday.
The undulating flight of one, the familiar landing,
the display flights of others against the horizon
flew me home to what's left standing, what's gone,
all that still flutters in the wet spring somewhere
behind my eyes. I couldn't hear the song that goes
with the display with the windows rolled up,
air conditioner on, but no matter, a brave recording
from another time is tucked away in the attic of a house
I thought I owned, but must be renting.
So many Bobolinks sharing one field might suggest
a lack of native habitat, but it was something
in their flight path, the depth
of blue between their wings and the hunched hay
that made me shudder.
Even the abandoned buildings, most windowless,
without paint, some with porches leaning, reminded me
a group of Bobolinks is a chain, and any chain that dark
can pull you through a mud hole and back again.
Hooked to a frame
wheeled over centuries, a vehicle of uncertain purpose
drags everything out, driven, some might say,
by the same spirit that settled
the prairie, but abstracts like that mean little
as elevators burn. Few live here anymore.
A semi and grain trailer parked on the southwest end.
Curtains here. A couple satellite dishes there.
The odd visitor like me, driving around,
at a loss without my reflection
gazing back from someone else's front room window,

before heading back the way I came, past a being
with black underparts, a creamy nape and white scapulars,
that claims territory with a bubbling song and settles right in.

GRID

Heat waves over the blacktop.
A cop hits the lights, stops
a van. Alberta plates.

Wild Rose Country, here we come
at a reasonable speed.
Traffic slows. Semis hauling

frozen meat to Humboldt,
cattle to auction in Saskatoon,
wheat to the terminal,

lumber to god knows
where, gear down.
Cars and trucks and bikes

close gaps. Brakes squeal.
A vehicle turns away,
heads down the grid.

The dust it raises hangs
as one would expect
on a day like this.

TRIPOD

You must be sturdy enough to handle a spotting scope
and a crosswind.
Tubular legs, rack and pinion column, tension
control, and smooth central column movement make you
what you are: an investment.
Barely affordable. The observer will grip your left leg
with her left hand, your handle
with the right while gusts hammer the scope into her glasses,
glasses into the bridge of her nose. She'll scan. Her eyes water.
Hold still. Her two legs will lean into your three
while she zooms in
on a flock of Black-bellied Plovers resting as they do
on one leg on the far edge of the slough east of Gord's
then she'll pull back slightly when a Buff-breasted Sandpiper
struts into view. *A Buff-breasted Sandpiper! No way!*
The scope will jiggle as if trying to hold back a laugh
at your expense, but never mind (she won't),
for after years of looking a dark eye
will stand out against the buff just like the field guide says
and she'll recognize the bird as she would her own mother.
It's a lifer, as birders say, for the lifelist,
and you make it possible. She can't identify anything
at such a distance, on a wet year without true shores,
without proper optics supported atop adjustable titanium legs
like yours, positioned separately to make all still, square
on the most uneven terrain.

STANDING IN CANOLA

a fool might try to walk
through a yellow field

see a sun
in each petal   the universe
expanding in the leaves
dark matter   black holes

hear Bertha
army worms eating
their way to wings

we all live in a yellow sub-
par crop of our own
seeding

a fool might
get farther than I did

TO THOSE CONSIDERING A RETURN TO THE LAND

A hundred dollars will buy you
a hot stone massage
at a spa in Regina. Fine.
Out here, with farming
the way it is,
if you want to align and balance
your energy centres,
your best bet's to lie
down in July on the gravel
at 3 in the afternoon,
let the flies and ants
walk all over you.
Don't forget to bring wine
and the bag of stones
from the fridge. Serve only
once properly chilled,
precisely inclined.
When placed on key areas,
cool stones alleviate stress,
calm the mind, quiet
the endless opera of *why*.
Keep a towel nearby.
Never mind, your thin
skin will let you know when
your time is up.

CONSTELLATION

A bat lifts the weight of summer
off my shoulders, the night heavy after days of rain,
the smell of fish freshly pulled from surrounding lakes

finding a way through the stillness to town and entering
through the basement window, a window so small
we're forced to stand close, end up hugging, as we wait

to see another swoop. We can't tell if it's one bat or two
so we stand there as if knowing matters, the soft glow
of the streetlight an embrace not quite obscuring

the brightest stars, and as I look to the constellations
a bat passes between my eyes and Venus, bringing Galileo
to mind with a telescope that magnifies my past, ours,

the light years, the lunar phases, our heliocentric view
of each other; our window has become a universe
and the night our home.

BLACK TERNS

Black terns zigzag
        the slough to the sky
while we estimate
        the cost of a well,
            composting toilet,
solar panels,
            batteries,
                wind tower,
not to mention a house,
the wind in our mouths,
        the wings
            escaping our urbanity.
A tern eyes me
    on its way by
                        then
doubles back,
its flight reading
        like an EKG,
an arrhythmia,
a premature
            ventricular
                contraction
                    to be exact.
        When it dives
in my direction,
it croaks.

ENDANGERED

Pale, weighing 63 grams tops, as much as an egg
straight from the carton, or a yolk
separated and left in the cracked half-shell of the day,
the Piping Plover stands on the edge of a road that cuts,
like the black band across the bird's forehead, through
an alkali slough, stares us down, doesn't move,
as our 1200 kg car creeps toward it. Fly already,
move aside, I say, but the male stays put, the band
around its left leg a shackle attached to a chain of events
rendering its kind almost invisible.
A species at risk of ending
up in our grill brings us to a stop. With the car turned off,
we scan the rocks that keep the road from sinking.
A nest must be tucked in a depression close by
but we can't spot it, looking hard
at so many rocks makes the eyes water. I know
the female has snuck off; that's what she does
in response to a threat and what else are we?
Sometimes the plainest camouflage hides everything.
If the eggs are destroyed they'll re-nest,
but plovers have their limits. It's late already,
the breeding season nearly over. The male eyes us
then cocks its head and pecks at something. A beetle,
a mayfly, another hole in my knowledge?

BONE COULEE

I used to cultivate this field.
Inside me, a prairie girl's heart still
runs like a 573 V8 diesel.

The Massey 1500 sure could pull.
I never considered the steepness of the hill
once part of a buffalo range,

never thought what would happen if I turned
the wrong direction on that slope.
In the contours of the coulee I saw

the jaws of that wild man,
the man who'd look left, between lines.
The rocks were teeth, a glimpse of tongue.

Round after round, through the heat, I dreamed,
as larks flew out of my path,
and a Great Horned Owl, sunning in a bluff, eyed me.

Round after round, me in the tractor's cockpit, riding
over ruts and washouts in second range, second gear,
door rattling, seat shaking, engine running

at 3000 revs. I looked back through the dust
to see gulls feeding, plunging in
and out of my wake.

FLEDGLING

The young ravens are silent now, for now
the sun polishes their backs as they sleep
off whatever the adult brought them.
Last evening, as five of them walked across
the rock, their shadows linked them
in one tight line, a frown, the rock beneath
a grimace, their squawks a hell perhaps Blake
could handle, or Szumigalski, the likes of me
out of the question, for all I can do is cover
my ears and hum tunelessly, trusting the noise
will end once the young feed, and hum I did
until they took flight and their awkwardness
somehow carried them deep into the spruce.

JONES' PEAK

Another poet stood atop the peak and looked
into the wind, the past, threw her head back,
her words lost in the howling, and once silent
she peered down the throat of the cliff
at the rock, the inflamed uvula, as if about
to say *ah*, when a Violet-green Swallow rose
as if properly summoned, circled like a poem
with incalculable speed until the poet laughed,
then stretched out on a gust for a moment
while the wind, with a bow, pulled out a chair
on which the swallow sat down with a grace
lost on ordinary beings. It rested there a while,
directing its full attention elsewhere. The poet
followed the direction of its gaze yet in no time,
with a subtle incline of its head, the swallow was gone.

WHO GETS WHAT

Willows wig the slough. Pale clouds
languish on the surface.

A dragonfly taps my shoulder on its way by
just as a distant cousin did at the funeral.

I turn. Battles abound. In front of me
cattail the colour of coffee

on the kitchen table where
siblings clash over the estate.

There will be no happy endings.
Somewhere I read that

dragonflies use motion camouflage
to appear stationary when attacking

and defending territory.
I remain unmoved

as they engage and take off.
All jaws. Wings transparent. Torn. Over what?

LOCAL ANAESTHETIC

The creek cuts through
the land's wrinkles. Nip and tuck,

an inconspicuous incision.
If I squint just right, the sunset

becomes a bloody glove
on a plastic surgeon's hand.

Face it. Deeper issues
can be repositioned,

fatty tissue removed,
but the matter of aging remains.

Mid-life squeezes into an evening
the colour of the bridesmaid gown

in the back of the closet. Then
it's placental, the crying

faces of next of kin, flushed
and inconsolable, and I back away,

find a corner
that burns and leaves me numb.

VISITING HOURS

It's routine. When I enter I stop,
pump hand sanitizer into my palm,
rub and walk on.

Around the corner the familiar
shuffle of slippers,
squeak of wheels

against brakes. I've come to fear
what's coming. Static.
Pathogens. Rub well. Rub it in,

I brush past
a wheelchair, old woman
strapped in. Smell the alcohol.

I fear she'll grab my half-dry hand
like she did yesterday. Help me
find a way out.

STROKE

Someone passes by the window,
a shadow on the side rails,
how much her face reminds me of home.

As she sleeps, I imagine a coyote. Cougar.
You name it. Wonder
where hunger crouches.

Her facial droop resembles a hillside
in the distant past where I stood
filling my pail with saskatoons,

clouds heading east, herding their shadows,
on the hill where mule deer vanish
like years, one by one.

Sometimes, when spooked,
an entire herd would crash into the coulee,
steep and thick with brush, disappearing

into snowberry, hawthorn, chokecherry,
where predators wait downwind. Branches
snapping like bones, bones like branches.

WEBS IN THE GRAVEYARD

Spiders mind the webs they've spun
on each eroding cross.

Each night they rebuild
subtle traps, anchor them to lichen,

bait them with dew, and each morning
a fly, like this one, sticks.

In a snap the spider wraps it,
injects it, drags the bound body

up a silk thread, angling
over to the transverse beam.

Leaves it dangling.

LOVE, THE DANCE

Dance of the Dead, Albin Egger-Lienz, 1915.

Death leans on a shovel, grinning,
arm linked

with that of the first man. The last man
in line glances back at life and its clichés.

Is that longing on his face, or does he ask
what longing is? I feel the pull in the last man's

neck, his need for someone to watch
him go. The land is barren and no one follows.

Is the first man resigned to his fate, or blind
and axe in hand leaning into exhaustion?

Is it best just to go? Yes,
the raised left hand of the pale-faced

hunchback is striking, his grip relaxed, cupping
the butt of a rifle. Yet look down

at the right hand. It will not sway on this final march.
The fingers are four stone tablets, broken and paralyzed.

Acknowledgements

Earlier versions of some of these poems appeared in *Grain*, *Northern Poetry Review* and *The Malahat Review* and aired on CBC Radio One. Thank you to the editors.

Thanks to the Canada Council for the Arts and the Saskatchewan Arts Board for grants that supported the creation of this work.

Thanks to Tracy Hamon, Gerald Hill, and Zachariah Wells for their input and editing of earlier drafts of the manuscript; and to Annette Bower, Ariel Gordon, and Paula Jane Remlinger for their help and advice.

Thank you to Paul Wilson for editing the book and to Hagios Press for bringing it forth.

As always, thanks to Harvey Schmidt, the first reader of my work, and to my family.

Brenda Schmidt is a writer, visual artist, naturalist, and blogger based in Creighton, a mining town in northern Saskatchewan. Brenda grew up on a farm in the Coteau Hills of southwest Saskatchewan. A former nurse, Schmidt also has a BA in English from the University of Waterloo. She has lived in northern Saskatchewan for 26 years, where she has been active as a freelance reporter/photographer, birding columnist, and volunteer in a recycling centre.

Schmidt is the author of three previous books of poetry, *A Haunting Sun* (Thistledown, 2001), *More than Three Feet of Ice* (Thistledown, 2005), and *Cantos from Wolverine Creek* (Hagios, 2008). Her cross-genre book of essays and letter fragments, *Flight Calls*, is forthcoming from Kalamalka Press in 2012 as part of the Mackie Lecture and Reading Series.

Schmidt's paintings have hung in solo and group exhibitions in Saskatchewan and Manitoba. She was one of the artists featured in the book, *Celebrating Saskatchewan Artists* (Saskatchewan Arts Alliance, 2006).